Bloom
Inspiring Gardens

Gary Graham & Ciaran Flanagan

IDEΛ
PUBLICATIONS LTD

Contents

Bloom was originally devised as a showcase for Ireland's ornamental and amenity horticulture sectors; nursery stock production, garden design and construction.

Garden shows are a great way to inspire and inform, as many gardens can only be fully experienced when all the senses are engaged; sight, sound, scent, taste and touch. Visitors are invited to Bloom to meet Ireland's top garden designers and horticulturists in the beautiful surroundings of the Phoenix Park, Dublin. The show runs for 5 days spanning the Irish June Bank Holiday Weekend each year.

Celebrate

The Mellow Chords

Dragons' Den investor, Bobby Kerr with his wife Mary

Mick Kelly, Founder GIY, Keith Barry, Mentalist & Dave Curran, GIY

Donal Skehan

Neven Maguire

Catherine Fulvio

Former President of Ireland, Mary McAleese and Garden Designer, Paul Doyle

Bloom is a true celebration aimed at passionate gardeners and novices alike, filled with flowers, food and fun for all ages. Former President of Ireland, Mary McAleese, Bloom's patron for the first five years helped to mark Bloom's significance in Ireland's calendar of important events.

Top gardening experts, chefs, entertainers and celebrities shared their knowledge and passion with 90,000 visitors in 2011. Throughout the show there is particular emphasis placed on provenance and meeting the maker. This extends to plants, garden design, food, craft, entertainment and educational features.

Craft Council of Ireland Demonstrations

Lorcan Bourke, Bord Bia speaking to a school group at the Michelle Obama White House Garden

THE CHOCOLATE GARDEN OF IRELAND

IRISH
APPLES
"Jonagold"
30c each

Coriander
Fresh Growing

Bord Bia's remit extends to food, drink and horticulture and Bloom provides the perfect setting to showcase the best that Ireland has to offer the world. Fresh produce, artisan food, meats, fish, beverages and beers are sampled and enjoyed by passionate food-lovers. Many visitors treat themselves to fine-dining while others relax and picnic in the beautiful parkland demesne. Most will spend a full day or more at the show enjoying all that the beautiful 70 acre site has to offer.

Paul Woods, Kilmurry Nurseries with the Morning Ireland Team

TV and Radio Presenter Ella McSweeney

Marty Whelan and Garden Designer Sheena Vernon

No event in Ireland has the same colour or drama that is associated with this horticultural extravaganza. It is a media magnet attracting journalists from across the country and further afield. Despite economic challenges there is no gloom at Bloom. The combination of creativity, colour and closeness to nature combine to create a garden-party atmosphere.

Glamorous gardens provide the perfect backdrop for fashion lovers. So many iconic designs are inspired by plants and nature and the latest styles are fashioned side by side with the latest trends in garden design, new plants introductions and a plethora of new foods and product innovations.

Fashion gurus Brendan Courtney & Sonya Lennon with young fans

Bord Bia
Irish Food Board

Welcomes you to bloom

Best in Season Market

Love Irish Food

Farming For Life

Artisan Food Market

Bord Bia Chief Executive, Aidan Cotter accompanies Former President of Ireland, Mary McAleese and Dr. Martin McAleese with Show Manager, Gary Graham during the official opening and visit to the Food Village at Bloom 2011. Newly introduced, the village includes livestock, edible horticulture crops, the Chefs' Summer Kitchen and numerous farm, growing and food production features that highlight the importance of the food and drink sectors to the Irish economy.

Garden Designers: Oliver & Liat Schurmann

Boundaries are less important in a rural idyll, especially if your garden is blessed with dramatic sea or mountain views. In that situation most designers will advise you to 'borrow the landscape' or to frame the views with plants. Most importantly, never try to compete with natural beauty as you will most likely fail.

Enclose

Garden Designer: Frazer McDonogh

Garden Designers: Oliver & Liat Schurmann

However, more and more of us live in a town or city where the views might include next door's washing line, passing cars or pedestrians. Many gardens are framed with grey concrete block walls, or garish orange timber panels and overlooked by neighbours' windows. In this situation good boundary treatment is vital for privacy, a sense of enclosure and security. Good boundaries also provide a backdrop to show off your plants and garden features.

A sense of enclosure is possible without solid walls or timber panels. A glass wall with plants behind it, suggests a much bigger space beyond. Rustic woven panels, hand-made or shop-bought, pick up on the tropical planting style and the colour used in the circular decking which appears to float like giant Lilly pads.

Garden Designer: Niall Maxwell

Solid walls, if properly constructed, can last a life-time and afford the opportunity to transform a garden at the drop of a hat, with a new coat of paint and a change in colour.

And while your boundary treatment is often your biggest expense, remember that it is visible from day one and remains visible while you wait for plants to mature. When deciduous plants and perennials drop their leaves or retreat underground it still looks good.

Garden Designer: Deirdre Pender

However, not everyone lives in the suburbs and when the opportunity arises to link the garden with the surrounding fields a hurdle fence maintains a rustic feel. This light-touch landscaping allows the garden to flow seamlessly into the wider landscape and the landscape to flow seamlessly into the garden

Garden Designer: Jane McCorkell

At the far end of the rustic spectrum, a beautifully crafted timber wall, incorporating a window to plants beyond and enclosing a contemporary seating and dining area, creates the perfect outdoor room. For the gardener seeking sumptuous materials and style using natural materials, these boundaries are every bit as stylish as the furniture and wall décor.

These walls of rammed earth reinvent a traditional wall-building technique. Combined with a wall of natural stone and contemporary paving that leads to sand and the coast they appear to be part of nature yet man-made.

The aggregates used to construct the walls appear ephemeral like moving sand and yet solid and permanent.

Garden Designer: Ger Mullen

Garden Designer: Brian O'Hara

Concrete block walls are common in Irish cities and suburbs. Left un-rendered and unpainted they can make a small garden cell-like, dull and dreary. Often in the rush to hide these walls the opportunity is missed to introduce colour and interesting shapes and perspectives. The construction of more walls within the garden draws the eye into the space and makes the boundaries part of the experience; much more than a functional barrier between your garden and the one next door.

Garden Designer: Sheena Vernon.

Veronica gentinoides, Polygonum affine 'Darjeeling Red', Iris sibirica, Aquilega vulgaris, and the pom pom shrub Vibernum opulis.

For many of us, the plants in our gardens are the closest that we get to a natural green landscape on a regular basis. In show gardens, they elevate garden design above interior design and include the bonus of seasonal and lifelong change. That said, many plants at Bloom are chosen for their spectacular performance in early June. Planting densities and plant sizes may be increased to create a strong visual impact during the show. Nevertheless, designers are still judged on their plant associations and their ability to put plants together that share similar soil and growing requirements.

Plant

Campanula'Sarastro'
Kilmurry Nurseries

*A dry riverbed of
succulents under a
Mulberry Tree bordered
by Buxus sempervirens*

Garden Designer: Paul Doyle

*Nepeta 'Walkers Low', Armeria Maritima 'Splendens'
under Quercus robur and Carpinus Betulus 'Fastigiata'*

Garden Designer: Ronnie Nevin

The plants we choose for our gardens have a much greater impact than the furnishings we place in our homes. Plants create homes and food for wildlife, they absorb CO_2 and provide us with oxygen. Plants screen unsightly views, absorb noise and particulate pollution. Native Whitebeam (Sorbus aria) is one of the best trees at removing harmful particulates from the atmosphere in Ireland.

Trees provide shade, shelter and beauty and a connection with the natural world that we cannot recreate with man-made objects.

Hostas and Euphorbia

Cistus 'Little Miss Sunshine'

Bloom is the perfect shop window to launch new plants to the public. Cistus 'Little Miss Sunshine' was bred by a Kildare-based nursery and it is now sold widely throughout Ireland and the UK.

Plant enthusiasts visit Bloom as early as possible each year to snap up new and interesting plant varieties that are grown by the 40 plus specialist nurseries who exhibit in the magnificent Floral Marquee.

Producing plants on a larger scale for world-wide sales, FitzGerald Nurseries from Kilkenny uses Bloom show gardens to exhibit their latest plant introductions such as this new black Phormium.

Phormium Black Adder

Knautia macedonica
'Melton pastels'

Stipa
tenuissima

Hosta "Shade
Fanfare"

Kilmurry Nurseries

Dicentra
'Bacchanal'

Iris sibirica
'Sparkling Rose'

Aquilegia 'Barlows White' with
Digitalis, and hostas

Garden Designer: Jane McCorkell

Philip Bankhead
Peninsula Primulas

Bloom's Floral Marquee hosts the most breathtaking and diverse display of plants for sale in Ireland. It is here that the spotlight is placed on individual plants and their unique qualities. In addition to purchasing new plant introductions, visitors have an opportunity to compare and contrast plants among their peers, their plant family, genus or species.

The nurseries are judged by a panel of internationally recognised judges and medals are awarded with the same rigorous scrutiny as that applied to the show gardens.

EREMURUS ROBUSTOS

AMBASADOR

EREMURUS ROMANCE

ALLIUM GLOBEMASTER

ALLIUM ATROPURPUREUM

NECTARSCORDUM

NEW SNOWBALL

Devines Allium Nursery

Betula pendula/pubescens
(Silver Birch) underplanted with
Ajuga reptans (Bugle) Allium
ursinum (Wild Garlic/Ramsons)
Athyrium filix femina (Lady Fern)
Deschampsia cespitosa
(Tufted Hairgrass).
Dryopteris filix-mas (Male Fern)
Galium odoratum (Sweet Woodruff)
Luzula sylvatica (Great Woodrush)
Polystichum setiferum
(Soft shield fern) and
Sagina subulata (Irish moss)

Garden Designer: Fiann Ó Nualláin

Felicia amelloides 'Reads Blue' Carex
ripara with Agapanthus 'Peter Pan'
in the background with Hedera helix
trained as a green screen

Garden Designer: Anne Hamilton

Garden Designer: Tim Austen

What we put underfoot determines how and when a garden can be used. The mild and damp conditions that keep our grass green and our trees growing tall require us to create surfaces that are well-drained and robust. Special care is called for when using decking or smooth surfaces and anti-slip treatments are always an option in situations that call for extra safety.

Walk

Garden Designer: Gary Foran

Concrete paving products are available in an almost limitless range of shapes and sizes. A skilled designer can create patterns and curves that follow the shape of seats and wall decoration. The use of loose pebble infill speeds drainage and new materials such as resin-bonded gravel maintain a 'natural' look while fixing aggregates in place.

Not all concrete is grey or brown. The use of a bright blue dye in the concrete slabs creates a lively and unusual colour. The contrast between it and the composite decking material is striking.

Garden Designer: Tim Austen

Intricate hand-made paving slabs in a traditional Suzhou garden style, dating back to the Ming Dynasty.

Garden Designers: Qin Huang & Libo Han

The random spacing of concrete strips forces the garden visitor to walk carefully through the closely-spaced trees.

Paving materials are used to slow the journey and ensure that the garden experience is magnified. Paving can be a thing of beauty. This group of individually cast linear pavers catch light and shade creating a focal point in the garden.

Garden Designer: Niall Maxwell

Paving products can be used in many combinations and with the greatest of formality or with a 'home-made' rustic finish.

The following pages capture some of the many treatments used in Bloom show gardens.

The use of composite decking is still in its infancy in Ireland but it is likely to increase. Its durability and non-slip qualities have already converted many to its benefits.

Whatever about the suitability of timber decking in our climate, there are many more who still favour it as their preferred material for a dining or relaxation space.

Naturally smooth stone and cobbles are pure luxury under bare feet and for the ultimate walking experience, bare feet on cool grass is impossible to beat for a path with little traffic.

Garden Designer: Paul Doyle

Garden Designers: Rita Higgins and Paul Quirke

Garden Designers: Oliver &

Garden Designer: Frazer McDonogh

Garden Designer: Paul Martin

Nothing whets the appetite nor adds more flavour to the meal than a warm breeze on a summer's evening. Enjoying good food and drink in the company of friends and loved ones in the garden was once a continental pastime but no longer.

The dining area may be covered or open to the stars, the food prepared close-by or served from the house. Whatever time and space dictates, there is always an outdoor dining solution.

Dine

The increasing demand for locally-sourced food and home-grown produce highlights the growing awareness of taste and provenance. Cooking skills requiring the combination of fresh ingredients and the investment of time and attention are being rediscovered. The appreciation of good food and how to get the most from high quality ingredients is greatly enhanced when the cooking experience is taken outdoors under the sun or the moonlight.

Garden Designer: Paul Martin

The optimal positioning of cooking equipment and dining space is a pre-requisite to ensure that the garden owner can benefit from sunny aspects or sheltered spaces.

Gardens designed for al fresco living often incorporate a number of dining areas. Breakfast can be eaten in one space, lunch in another and evening meals in yet another; all catching the sun as it moves around a garden.

Garden Designers: Gary Hanaphy & Colm Quinn

Garden Designer: Colm Doyle

Water is elemental and used well in a garden it can add as much to the experience as fantastic plants. Water, plants and rock provide the strongest links to the natural world.

However, only water can provide the same soothing sounds of rustling leaves, the movement associated with wind or the reflective qualities of a still lake or calm ocean.

Splash

Garden Designers: Rita Higgins and Paul Quirke

Our temperate maritime climate ensures a plentiful supply of water that can be incorporated into interesting and environmentally-sustainable water features.

The use of small stepping stones across water adds interest and excitement on the journey to an inviting hammock. The inky blackness of the surrounding water and 'naturalistic' use of water plants suggests a tropical setting in keeping with the overall design and atmosphere.

Garden Designer: Frazer McDonogh

Garden Designer: Paul Martin

This reflective canal forms the backbone of a strong symmetrical design and visitors are forced to cross it a number of times on their journey to the destination dining room at the bottom of the garden.

The rusted steel edge is a contemporary treatment and the designer has allowed for deeper water levels and shade from sun to accommodate Koi Carp. Fish add more movement and another point of interest in the garden.

Garden Designer: Paul Martin

Garden Designers: Oliver and Liat Schurmann

Garden Designer: Anthony Ryan

Nothing catches light like water, whether still or moving. While few of us take the time to observe the movement of clouds or sun across the sky, a large body of still water magnifies the beauty of surrounding plants, interesting architecture and all that moves or flies.

The soothing sound of water gushing or gurgling is the most pleasing disguise for traffic or city noise.

Water used to its best to create an exotic and almost swamp-like atmosphere. The darker the better to create a natural mirror that draws the sky into the garden.

Garden Designers: Peter Little with Rita Higgins & Paul Quirke

An atypical garden where water takes on the central role and the plants are pushed to the perimeter. A sunken seating area at the centre approached by a natural stone bridge that sits just below water level creates the most intriguing of spaces.

When visitors are seated at the centre the water is almost at eye level, providing the lucky guest with a unique perspective on the surrounding garden. The use of natural plant filters and a slow but constant flow towards the centre keeps the surface of the water clear of leaves and plant debris.

Garden Designers: Oliver and Liat Schurmann

This tribute to the dramatic water features at Mount Usher Gardens in County Wicklow was so well constructed that numerous visitors to the show assumed that the designer had constructed his garden around a naturally occurring fast-flowing stream.

In fact he started with a green field site. While all gardens, with or without water, are in some way 'artificial', a skilled designer can create an idyllic space that feels more 'natural' than nature.

Garden Designer: Tim Austen

Gardens can provide stimulation for both body and mind. In fact, such are the benefits that they are often referred to as a 'green gym'. Garden design, construction and maintenance all require some level of physical or mental exertion. The shaping of a border, the pruning of a plant and the growing of fruit and vegetables requires creativity and contemplation. The Garden can be enjoyed by the whole family where all ages can partake in outdoor games and sports.

Play

The young mind can create adventure and excitement that is not always accessible to adults. This is achievable, even in the smallest and simplest of outdoor spaces.

A good garden designer will address issues of safety and security for children, but a great garden designer will also recognise the opportunities for 'natural' play areas or spaces that complement the 'designed' elements and features.

Garden Designer: Mark O'Loughlin

Garden Designer: Mark O'Loughlin

Only in a garden or outdoor space can children get up close and personal with birds and insects, plants and water.

We want the best for our children and the garden is a great provider of fresh air which revitalises both body and mind. Remember that the garden is an oxygen-making machine.

Garden Designers: Carol Duffy and Donal Ryan

Garden Designers: Gary Hanaphy & Colm Quinn

Garden Designers: Paul & Orla Woods

A garden can provide the healthy benefits of sensible sun exposure. Vitamin D, the sunshine vitamin, is a hormone made by skin exposed to sunlight which has been shown to act as a powerful inhibitor of abnormal cell growth. Sunshine is also a mood enhancer.

Garden Designer:Colm Doyle

The human eye can perceive more shades of green than of any other colour. Green triggers a response in the sympathetic nervous system that relieves tension in the blood vessels and lowers blood pressure. At some level in our subconscious we all know this and consequently we are drawn to spaces surrounded by green. When we get to this 'green' destination in the garden we can escape to a safer place.

Escape

Garden Designer: Anne Hamilton

Something in our make-up, perhaps our survival instincts or our origin in the womb compels us to seek a 'safe' place to sit and rest. No matter how great the view to the front, it is always comforting to sit in an enclosure and survey the beauty as a watcher rather than the watched. This 'safe' place if glimpsed from the house can draw a visitor in search of 'sanctuary'.

Garden Designer: Lurene Fitzpatrick

Garden Designers: Marion Keogh, Bernie Torpey & Una Thomas
in collaboration with Róisín de Buitléar

Construction can be simple or functional, a raised garden room provides a vantage point for views over the flowering plants and glass sculptural pieces below. Glass panels in the base allow uninterrupted appreciation of the small stream that flows beneath.

The black netting used for cladding provides dappled shade and shelter from the breeze. An unusual choice of cladding material that links perfectly with the honey-bee and bee-keeping theme.

Garden Designers: Naomi Coad-Maenpaa & Miriam Matthews

Why escape to a hotel sauna when you can create one in your garden? With the outdoor shower and seated area close by, the garden owner can dry their hair au naturel while enjoying a planting palette inspired by the Burren.

This Scandinavian-inspired garden reduced its carbon footprint by using a wood-burning stove to heat the water and the sauna and the waste water is naturally filtered through bog plants. Building the sauna with wood panels and roofing it with sedum adds to its eco-friendliness.

Garden Designers: Qin Huang & Libo Han

The dramatic flying roof
on the Ire-Su Garden draws
the eye to the heavens.

Garden Designer: Elma Fenton

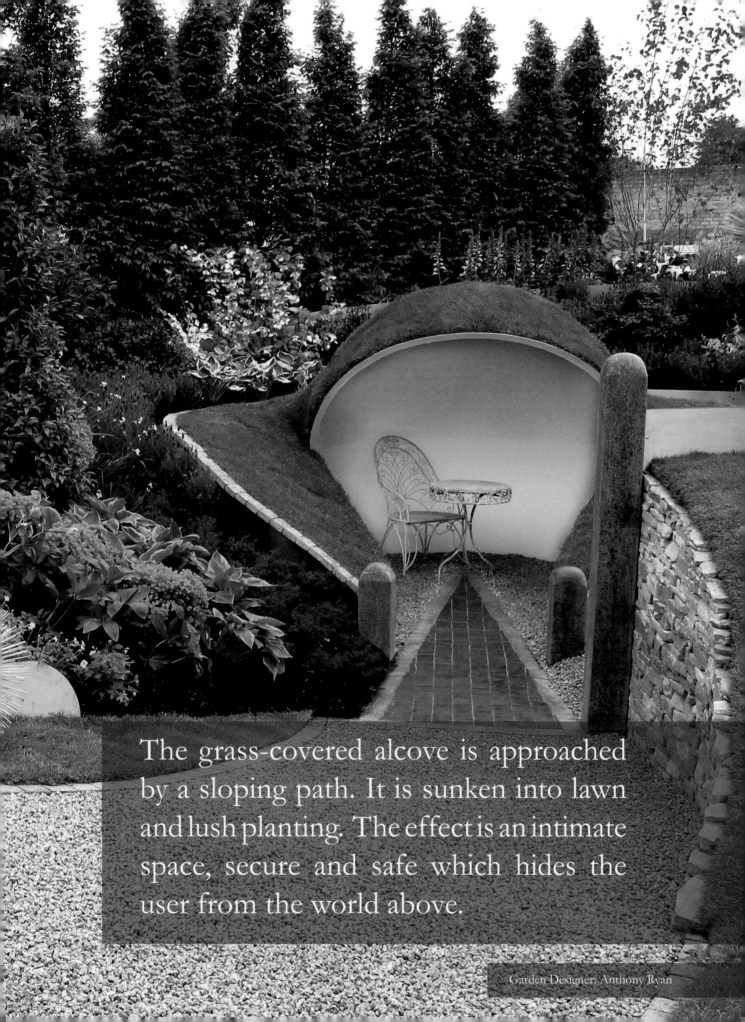

The grass-covered alcove is approached by a sloping path. It is sunken into lawn and lush planting. The effect is an intimate space, secure and safe which hides the user from the world above.

Garden Designer: Anthony Ryan

Garden Designer: Tim Austen

Garden Designer: Stephanie Charvatova with Anthony Ryan

A simple chair is all that is required to draw you out into the garden. If the path to the chair were a straight line it would be less seductive. Natural curiosity lures us around the curve towards the hidden step in the knowledge that we can claim the chair and view the garden from a slightly hidden but raised vantage point.

Garden Designer: Ken Byrne

This handmade nest-like structure was inspired by a desire to communicate the importance of 'home' and the scourge of 'homelessness'.

The organic form is so unpretentious it resonates at a level far deeper than subjective opinion on style or colour. It defines home perfectly: a place to be safe.

Garden Designer: Stephen Dennis

A glass box in the garden; is there a better way to enjoy all that the garden has to offer?

An escape that provides shelter from rain is a great addition to any Irish garden. It will draw you from the house even on the wettest of days and at the coldest of times. Even the journey to and from the covered area provides an experience not attainable from the house.

The garden is always changing and close inspection throughout the year affords an opportunity to spot emerging shoots and flower buds or leaves and twigs starting to change their colour. The scents and sounds of a well planted garden cannot be enjoyed from a distant window.

Garden Designer: Peter Donegan

Garden Designers: Morag Kelly, Svaja Vaičiulevičiūte and Jane Fitzgerald White

Gardens have become a laboratory and a shop window for designers with an interest in environmental sustainability. Recent economic changes have stimulated greater creativity and innovation in the search for affordable solutions. As Bloom gardens are less encumbered by the constraints associated with domestic gardens, designers can experiment, educate and provide numerous examples of sustainable gardening and living.

Sustain

Garden Designer: Sheena Vernon

The ways in which a show garden can incorporate and champion sustainable ideas are too many to list or photograph and this section provides a small selection; use of insect-loving plants, recycled furniture, glass bottle edging, 'bug hotels', using asthma-friendly plants and a cob oven under a sedum-covered roof that captures rain water and slowly releases it down chains into swales that reduce flooding.

Garden Designers: Institute of Technology Blanchardstown

Garden Designer: Fiann Ó Nualláin

The inclusion of wildlife benefits everyone; grateful birds, butterflies and buzzing bees add life, movement and music to a garden.

Garden Designers: Rita Higgins and Paul Quirke

Home-production of fruit and vegetables championed by the 'Grow-It-Yourself' organisation has taken root in communities, schools and back-gardens nationwide.

At Bloom, garden designers highlight creative and aesthetic opportunities while celebrating the beauty of edible plants. 'Companion planting' where ornamental flowering plants are combined with edible plants is a great way to attract pollinators and predator insects. They eat the ones that eat your vegetables!

Garden Designers: Paul and Orla Woods

Show me your garden and I'll tell you who you are

A natural swimming pond relies on the use of plants to filter the water 'organically' without the use of chemicals.

A perfect blend of cutting-edge garden design and environmental sensitivity.

Garden Designer: Elma Fenton

If evidence were required that edible gardens can be both productive and beautiful, this garden has it in spades. The box hedging provides year-round structural interest while the vegetable patch rests in the winter and the bright paint colours and architectural features look great whatever the season or the weather.

The storage area is hidden and the terracotta rhubarb forcers and scarecrow add a bit of old world nostalgia.

Garden Designer: James McConnell

This courtyard garden was designed to show that rainwater harvesting can be both environmentally sound and visually appealing.

Rain water is collected from roof and hard surfaces and stored in an underground rain water harvesting unit where it can be used indoors and outdoors in a variety of ways.

As rainwater travels down the hanging chains it catches the light and entertains the visitor.

Garden Designer: Jane McCorkell

Garden Designer: Sophie Von Maltzan

This outdoor gallery was designed and constructed using a minimalist approach and on a shoe-string budget. The focus in this design is on the artwork and not on the gallery.

The materials chosen reflect the designer's commitment to minimising the economic or environmental impact of the installation. Everything is low cost, recycled and reused post show.

Garden Designer: Tim Austen

Some garden designers abhor the term 'outdoor room' as they truly believe that a garden can be so much more than a functional or attractive room outside. Furthermore, plants and nature need little in the way of decoration. However, in the same way that interesting architecture provides a visual focal point, so too does art, sculpture and well-designed furniture in a garden. An arresting form or shape, whether man-made or God-made, can excite, calm or inspire.

Decorate

What better place than the garden for artists, craft-workers and furniture-makers to strut their stuff? Whether shop-bought or commissioned and custom-made, changing seasons and changing light add a layer of interest that cannot be recreated in an interior space.

For many artists the garden is a green canvas, an outdoor gallery where plants are used as the foil for works of art. Which comes first, the garden or the art? It hardly matters if the end result is beauty beyond the confines of design.

Garden Designer: Tim Austen

Garden Designer: Paul Doyle

Garden Designer: Jack Harte

Giant plants that bloom all year long. Made from scrap metal, these giant flowers bring a smile to the face of young and old. Artists and garden designers can combine their talents to create humourous outcomes.

This artist turned designer challenges us to find the distinction between art and garden. Through the use of a number of artistic media that exploit natural light and offer up different experiences and perspectives as the sun moves across the sky we are captivated by vivid colour, shadow and reflected movement.

Garden Designer: Dawn Aston

Garden Designers: Marion Keogh, Bernie Torpey & Una Thomas
in collaboration with Róisín de Buitléar

Garden Designer: Dawn Aston

Garden Designer: Paul Martin

Art in its many guises offers inspiration for gardens and a poem by W.B Yeats 'In the Seven Woods' provided the theme for this beautifully handcrafted garden. Shaping the seating and paving into a clearly defined pattern ensures that this courtyard sanctuary is appreciated from the surrounding windows and most especially the windows above.

Garden Designer: Ger Mullen

Garden Designer: Colm Doyle

Garden Designer: Maryann Harris

Garden Designer: Paul Martin

Garden Designer: Jane McCorkell

Garden Designer: Anthony Ryan

Garden Designer: Hugh Ryan

This installation was designed to hold people's attention long enough to introduce them to an alternative, forward-looking approach to the use of outdoor space.

The designer posits that while garden tradition is important, it cannot remain static. The boldness in choice of colour and materials provides a welcome and effective contrast to other design approaches.

These suspended escape pods combine engineering, environmental science, horticulture, sculpture, blacksmithing and garden design in their construction. Each pod is wired for sound, fuelled by solar energy and the lucky escapee can enjoy his or her favourite tunes in a secluded, floating world of green.

Garden Designer: Peter Little with Rita Higgins & Paul Quirke

Why not make the most of the creative flair and technical genius that is available to you from Ireland's award-winning garden designers? Choose from a short consultation, a simple sketch or a full 'design and build' service. You may prefer to use your green fingers to bring your own concepts to fruition. That's fine too. The ideas in this book are yours to use and yours to translate to your garden. However, if you want to create an Inspiring Garden of your own the best place to start is with an inspiring garden designer.

Here follows a comprehensive list of Bloom's garden designers with their contact details for your convenience. Every photograph of a Bloom garden carries the garden designers name. If a specific piece of art or item of furniture takes your fancy please contact the garden designer for more information.

Design

Alphabetical list of Garden Designers with gardens at Bloom 2007-2011

Billy Alexander

Email: billy@dicksonia.ie   Web: www.kellsgardens.ie   Tel: +353 (0)87 777 6666
2011   Kells Bay Garden - With Frazer McDonagh *Sponsor: Viking*

Monica Alvarez

Email: monica.alvarez@cfedundrum.ie / info@baumannlanscapes.ie
Tel: +353 (0)86 1003207
2007   The Mosaic Garden (Contractor: Baumann Landscapes)

Dawn Aston

Email: info@dawnaston.co.uk   Web: www.dawnaston.co.uk   Tel: +44 771 708 1877
2009   An Artist's Retreat
2010   Urban Oasis - With Crawford Leitch

Tim Austen

Email: designdesk@austenassociates.ie   Web: www.austenassociates.ie
Tel: + 353 (0)86 805 7343 / + 353 (0)404 66433
2008   Inspiration from Mount Usher *Sponsor: Plants & Planters*
2009   The Garden Lounge *Sponsor: Grangemore Plants and Double L Concrete*
2010   The VSO Dollar-A-Day Garden *Sponsor: The VSO*
2011   The Growise Garden *Sponsor: Growise, Bord Na Móna and Kildare Growers*

Colin Brady

Email: info@urbanlandscapedesign.ie   Web: www.urbanlandscapedesign.ie
Tel: +353 (0)87 957 4614 / +353 (0)1 298 2250
2008   Serenty *Sponsor: Brady Property Management*   (Contractors: Urban Landscape Design)

**Leanne Brennan, Ruth Turpin
& Aoife Power**

Email: wildandgreenbloom2011@gmail.com   Tel: +353 (0)86 071 6970
2011   Wild and Green

Ken Byrne

Email: ken.byrne@msn.com   Web: www.kenbyrnedesign.weebly.com   Tel: +353 (0)86 0579648
2011   Supergarden *Sponsors: Woodie's DIY & Growise, Bord Na Móna*

Stephanie Charvato

With Anthony Ryan
2011   The Outdoor Living Garden *Sponsor: Woodie's DIY & Garden Centre, Carrickmines*

Owen Chubb

Email: info@owenchubblandscapers.com   Web:www.ownchubblandscapers.com
Tel: +353 (0)87 2306 128 / +353 (0)1 492 0904
2007   The Fáilte Ireland Garden *Sponsor: Fáilte Ireland*

Brian Cleary

Email: briancleary01@gmail.com   Web: www.cfedundrum.com   Tel: +353 (0)86 100 3207
2011   Columbarium *Sponsor: CFE Dundrum*

Naomi Coad-Maenpaa
& Miriam Matthews

Email: naomicoad@yahoo.com / miriammatthews@oceanfree.net
Tel: +353 (0)87 241 2883 /+353 (0)51 29 1195
2007   **Baltic to Burren**

Laurence Colleran

Email: lcolleran@sdublincoco.ie   Web:www.sdcc.ie Tel: +353 (0)1 414 9000
2008   **The Blooming Good Fun School Garden**

James Comiskey

Email: jamescomiskey@vodafone.ie Tel: +353 (0)87 7817178 / +353 (0)43 83196
2009   **About Your Garden**
2010   **Recess**
2011   **Going Forward**   *Sponsor: LifeFibre Co.*

Damien Costello

& The Customers of Focus Ireland
Email: DeirdreConnolly@focusireland.ie Web: www.focusireland.ie Tel: +353 (0)86 835 0098
2011   **A Place of Belonging**   *Sponsor: Focus Ireland*

Edward Cullen & Sarah Richter

Email: info@amazongardendesign.ie Web: www.amazongardendesign.ie
Tel: +353 (0)85 730 5997 / +353 (0)1 406 0004
2010   **Floresta Amazônica**

Dominick Cullinane

Email: info@dominickcullinanelandscapes.com Web:www.dominickcullinanelandscapes.com
Tel: +353 (0)86 3345071
2009   **Aubergine**

Stephen Dennis

Email: stephendennisdesigns@gmail.com   Web: www.stephendennisdesigns.com
Tel: +353 (0)85 123 6535 / + 353 (0)1 807 1687
2007   **The Berlin Wall Garden**
2010   **Breathe**

Peter Donegan

Email: info@doneganlandscaping.com Web: www.doneganlandscaping.com
Mob: +353 (0)87 659 4688 Tel: +353 (0)1 8028712
2007   **No Rubber Soul**
2008   **Le Jeux De L'Amour** *Sponsor: Gormleys Fine Art*

Bernadette Doran

Email: garden9@eircom.net Tel: +353 (0)87 2511498
2007   **Relections of Nature in Time and Space**   **- With Eamonn Doran**

Eamonn Doran

Email: gardenplanning@eircom.net   Tel: +353 087 9726824
2007   **Relections of Nature in Time and Space**   **- With Bernadette Doran**
2008   **Mission Impossible.....Mission Accomplished! - With Catherine Gallagher**
    Sponsor: A2Z Landscape Planning

Gerry Doran & Pam O'Shea Email: gerrydoran@hotmail.com Web: www.greenexpectations.ie
Tel: +353 (0)87 958 1863 / +353 (0)1 836 7438
2008 **Drama in Bloom** *Sponsor: ESB Independent Energy*

Rachel Doyle Email: arboretum@eircom.net Web: www.arboretum.ie Tel: +353 (0)59 972 1558
2007 **Absolute Garden**

Paul Doyle Email: info@pauldoyledesign.com Web: www.pauldoyledesign.com Tel: +353 (0)86 263 8985
2008 **'Wherever the Wind Takes Me I Travel'** *Sponsor: The Travel Department*
2010 **Eclipse 2010** *Sponsor: Specsavers*

Colm Doyle Email: info@doylescapes.ie Web: www.doylescapes.ie
Tel: +353 (0)87 617 2641/+353 (0)1 204 8020
2008 **R n'R** Designer-Colm Doyle & Dean Lacey *Sponsor: Doylescapes*
2009 **Urban Native** Designer-Colm Doyle & Dean Lacey
2010 **G&T** Designer-Colm Doyle, Sean Doyle & Dean Lacey

Carol Duffy & Donal Ryan Email: donal@dhryan.ie Web: www.ippa.ie / www.dhryan.ie
Tel: +353 (0)86 835 4336/+353 (0)1 463 0010 / +353 (0)50 42 8850
2010 **IPPA Nature's Playground of Possibilities** *Sponsor: IPPA & DH Ryan Architects*

Billy Fahy Email: billy_fahy@hotmail.com Web: www.botaniclandscapes.com Tel: +353 (0)87 647 5256
2008 **Billy's Botanica** *Sponsor: Institute of Technology Blanchardstown*

Elma Fenton Email: info@ellenlandscapedesigns.com www.elmafenton.ie
Tel: +353 (0)86 812 2396 / 01 497 7311
2007 **Harmony With Nature…Every Little Helps** *Sponsor: Tesco Ireland*
2008 **Garden Revival - The Finest…** *Sponsor: Tesco Ireland*

Sinéad Finn Email: mail@sineadfinn.com Web: www.sineadfinn.com
Tel: +353 (0)1 842 1768 / (0)87 989 0910
2007 **Haven**
2008 **The Spaces Between** (Contractor: Advance Lanscape Services)
2010 **Kilsaran Lifestyle Garden** *Sponsor: Kilsaran*

Caroline Fitzpatrick **2011** **The Contemporary Garden** *Sponsor: Woodie's DIY & Garden Centre, Swords*

Lurene Fitzpatrick Email: lurenefitz@msn.com Tel: +353 (0)86 170 9298
2008 **What a Wonderful World We Live in!** (Contractor: Birchall Landscaping)
2009 **The Jewel Garden** *Sponsor of Plants: dyg.ie* (Contractor: Birchall Landscaping)

Gary Foran

Email: info@garywforan.ie   Web: www.garywforan.ie   Tel: +353 (0)86 350 8845
2007   **A Space Within**
2009   **Harmonium**

Catherine Gallagher

Email: catherinegallagher08@eircom.net   Tel: +353 (0)87 818 1284
2008   **Mission Impossible…..Mission Accomplished! - With Eamonn Doran**
Sponsor:A2Z Landscape Planning

Grace Garde & Paul Kavanagh

Email: grace_garde@hotmail.com   Web: www.landscape.ie
2007   **Bizzy Bee Children's Maze Garden** *Sponsor: Boyne Valley*

Mark Grehan

Email: mark@markgrehandesigns.com   Web: www.markgrehandesigns.com Tel: 087 271 1277
2008   **Inís Óirr** *Sponsor:Gardenworks*   (Contractor: Broomfield Landscapes)

Robert Guinness

Email: rcg@steammuseum.ie   Web: www.steam-museum.ie   Tel: +353 (0)87 827 1435
2011   **The Steam Museum Garden With Sophie Von Maltzan**
Sponsor: Steam Museum & Park Lodge Walled Garden

Anne Hamilton

Email: anneh@foxgardens.com Web: www.foxgardens.com
Tel: +353 (0)86 315 7114 /023 884 7170
2010   **Islands** *Sponsors: Ballymaloe Country Relish, Dubliner Cheese, Camden Court Hotel & Life Fibre*
2011   **The Orb** *Sponsor: Glenisk*

Gary Hanaphy & Colm Quinn

Email: Gary@landscapestudiosireland.com   Web: www.landscapestudiosireland.com
Tel: +353 (0)85 191 6698
2010   **Be Stylish, Your Way** *Sponsor: Quinny*
2011   **The Hidden Cube Style Garden** *Sponsor: Arnotts*

Maryann Harris

Email: maryann.harris@dublincity.ie   Tel: +353 (0)87 656 1676
2011   **Riverrun - UNESCO City of Literature Garden** *Sponsor: Dublin City Council*

Jack Harte

Email: jackmyharte@hotmail.com   Web: www.hartedesigns.ie   Tel: +353 (0)87 413 3595
2011   **An Adventure with Thumbelina**

Rita Higgins & Paul Quirke

Email: info@anugreen.ie   Web: www.anugreen.ie   Tel: +353 (0)86 351 1836 /021 477 8615
2009   **Ag Cur Baistí**
2010   **The Upper End...'**
2011   **Portach** - With Peter Little, Hortisculptures

John Hogan

Email: Dunsanyland@hotmail.com Tel: + 353 1 836 1629
2008   **Garden 1** *Sponsor: Tesco Ireland & Dublin Meath Growers*

Liz Houchin

Email: info@lizhouchindesign.com Web: www.lizhouchindesign.com   Tel: +353 (0)87 997 0789
2007   **What's in a Name?**

Qin Huang & Libo Han

15 Jinpu Road, Industrial Zone, Suzhou, P.R. China
2011   **Ire-Su Garden**

Morag Kelly, Svaja VaicIuleviciute Tel: 087 940 6326
and Jane Fitzgerald White   2008   **A View Askew**   *Sponsor: Senior College Dún Laoghaire*

Maximilian Kemper

Email: kemper_maximilian@yahoo.de Tel: +353 (0)85 121 1108
2008   **How does your garden go?**
2009   **LifeFibre Co. ECOlogic** Sponsor: LifeFibre Co.

Anne Kennedy

Email: akennedy@eircom.net Web: www.theonionshed.com
Tel: +353 (0)87 247 8751 / +353 (0)42 937 3032
2007   **Wirestring Quartet**

Marion Keogh, Bernie Torpey Email:3DesignGardens@gmail.com Web: www.3designgardens.ie Tel: +353 (0)87 813 7718
& Una Thomas   2009   **5x5 In The City**   **With the College of Further Education Dundrum**
2010   **Beauty & The Bees**   **With Róisín de Buitléar** *Sponsor: Burt's Bees*

Kerry Earth Education Project Email: earthedkerry@gmail.com Tel: +353 (0)87 924 6968 / +353 (0)66 7137011
Oideachtas Ón Dúlra   2008   **The Living Classroom, Organic Food Production & Bio-diversity in Schools**
Sponsor: Department of Agriculture, Fisheries & Food
2009   **The Living Classroom Recycled**

Ciarán Kirwan

Email: Ciaran.kirwan@meadow.ie Web: www.meadow.ie
Tel: +353 (0)1 406 3034 / +353 (0)86 866 7599
2008   **Ford Allergy Friendly Garden** *Sponsor: Ford*
2009   **The Cheese Garden** *Sponsor: CÁIS The Association of Irish Farmhouse Cheesemakers*

Max Lim

Email: info@tgireland.com Web: www.tgireland.com Tel: +353 (0)87 991 1618 / (0)91 738 102
2007   **Five Senses Garden** - **With James Kilkelly (assistant designer)**

Peter Little

Email: hortisculpture@gmail.com Web:www.hortisculptures.com Tel: +353(0)86 238 7069
2011   **Portach** With Rita Higgins & Paul Quirke

Dominic Loughran

Email info@dreamgardens.ie   Web www.dreamgardens.ie
Tel: +353 (0)1 624 9612 / +353 (0)87 2854602
2009   Life in a Shack

Barry Lupton

Email: barlupton@gmail.com   Tel: +_353 (0)86 349 2286
2007   Agraria *Sponsor: North Dublin Growers*

Paul Martin

Email: info@paulmartindesigns.com   Web: www.paulmartindesigns.com
Tel: +353 (0)87 689 4759   + 353 (0)42 935 7344
2007   Dragonflies & Flutterbies *Sponsor: Pfizer*
2007   Orchard Home & Garden *Sponsor: Orchard Home & Garden*
2007   A Tuscan Paradise *Sponsor: Scalpwood Nurseries*
2008   Pfizer Health & Wellness Garden *Sponsor: Pfizer*

Susan Maxwell

Email: sdmaxwell@eircom.net   Tel: +353 (0)87 263 7341 / +353 (0)1 497 8624
2007   Oasis

Niall Maxwell

Email: niallmaxwellgardens@gmail.com   Web: www.niallmaxwellgardens.ie
Tel: +353 (0)86 358 9611
2009   Weekend Review
2010   Victus Ortus

James McConnell

Email: jfjmcconnell@gmail.com   Tel:+353 (0)85 782 9966 /+353 (0)46 907 5824
2010   Urban Idyll *Sponsor: Woodie's DIY & Growise, Bord Na Móna (Super Garden)*

Jane McCorkell

Email: mccorkell_jane@yahoo.ie   Web:www.janemccorkelllandscape.ie
Tel: +353 (0)87 6839520 / +353 (0)1 835 3181
2007   Keelings Naturally Fresh Show Garden *Sponsor: Keelings Naturally Fresh*
2008   The Orchard Path *Sponsor: Keelings Naturally Fresh*
2010   The Rain Garden *Sponsor: Sap Group*
2011   The VW 'Think Blue' Garden *Sponsor: Volkswagen*

Frazer McDonogh

Email: fmcdonogh47@gmail.com   Web: www.rockandwaterscapes.com
Tel: +353 (0)87 225 8220 / +353 (0)404 66795
2008   The Lyons Tea Garden "Green Retreat" *Sponsor: Lyons Tea*
2009   The Secluded Water Garden
2010   The Travel Department China Garden *Sponsor: The Travel Department*
2011   Kells Bay Garden (With Billy Alexander) *Sponsor: Viking*

**Breffni McGeough
& Francis Doyle**

Email: breffnidesign@gmail.com   Web: www.outerscapes.ie   Tel: +353 (0)86 217 1857
2011   Taken Out Of Context

**Leonie Meehan
& Pearce College**

Email: ltmeehan@eircom.net Web: www.pearsecollege.ie
Tel: +353(0)87 665 6896/ +353(0)53 938 9920
2008   Taking the right 'course' - Learning from Nature
Sponsor: Pearse College of Further Education

Gerard Mullen

Email: germullen@hotmail.com   Email: www.gerardmullen.com   Tel: 086 602 3284
2007   Inner Space
2008   Sandscape *Sponsor: Woodie's DIY*   (Contractor: Comeragh Landscaping)

Ronnie Nevin

With Landscape and Garden Design Students from Senior College Dun Laoghaire
Tel: +353 (0)1 2800385 / +353 (0)87 241 9219
2010   Patterns of Change...a window on the future   *Sponsor: Bord Bia*

**The Office of Public Works
Garden Team**

Web: www.phoenixpark.ie   Tel:+353 (0)1 821 3021
2007   In the Spirit of a Formal Victorian Walled Kitchen Garden *Sponsor: OPW*

Fiann Ó Nualláin

Email: info@inspiringgardens.ie   Web: www.inspiringgardens.ie
Tel: +353 (0) 87 315 4539/ 01 455 8900
2007   Resistance is Everything
2008   Cuimhne (memory/memorial)
2008   The Book of Welcomes Garden *Sponsor: Fáilte Ireland*
2009   The Great Escape *Sponsor: Unicef*
2009   Discover Ireland...Be Amazed *Sponsor: Fáilte Ireland*
2010   Behold I Bear Gifts
2010   The GIY Edible Garden *Sponsor: GIY Ireland*
2011   Treat not Trigger...the Asthma and Allergy Friendly Garden
          Sponsor: Asthma Society of Ireland

Rosa O'Connell

Email: info@rosaoconnell.ie   Tel: +353(0)86 600 2686 /+353 (0)21 4644 6682
2009   The Seven Woods *Sponsor: Woodies DIY & Growise, Bord Na Móna (Supergarden)*

**Peter O'Brien
& Sons Landscaping**

Email: peter@obrienlandscaping.com   Tel: +353 (0)1 245 2555
2010   The Green Igloo

Brian O'Hara

Email: brian.ohara@web.de   Email: www.projectgarden.ie
Tel: +353 (0) 87 6891679 / +353 (0)1 2311032
2007   Outspace 1 - Galleria
2008   Outspace #2 *Sponsors: Applegreen & Lavazza* (Contractor: Amazing Gardens)

Mark O'Loughlin

Email: markoloughlin@ireland.com   Web: www.sanctuarysynthetics.ie
Tel: +353 (0)86 8333255
2011   The Alice in Wonderland Sanctuary Garden *Sponsor: Sanctuary Synthetics*

Suzanne O'Neill	**2011**	**The Multifunctional Garden** - With Anthony Ryan

Sponsor: Woodie's DIY   & Garden Centre, Tallaght

Deirdre Pender

Email: talamhlandscapes@eircom.net   Web: www.talamhlandscapes.com
Tel: +353 (0)87 223 7287 / +353 (0)59 916 3757

2010   **Nemeton**
2011   **AOS Sí** (Contractor: Dan Morrisey Ltd & Dunnes Nurseries)

Gwen Reil

Email: gwenreil@gmail.com Tel: +353 (0)87 2436015

2007   **A Rooftop Retreat**

Anthony Ryan

Email: landscapearchitecture@eircom.net   Web: www.hayesryan.com
Tel: +353 (0) 86 063 0552 / +353 (0) 59 862 6093

2007   **The Glasshouse Effect**   *Sponsors: Kildare Growers*
           (Contractor: Hayes Ryan Landscape Architecture)
2009   **Metamorphosis**
           Sponsors: Bord Na Móna, Hayes Ryan Landscape Architecture, Kildare Growers

---

Hugh Ryan

Email: mail@hughryan.ie Tel: +353 (0) 87 256 1139 /+353 (0) 4024 1841

2009   **Sequia**

Jule May Schedwill
& David Everard

Email: julieschedwill@eircom.net   Web: www.everardlandscapes.ie
Tel: +353 (0)87 412 4993 / +353 (0) 402 37671

2008   **Mystical Woodland Retreat** *Sponsor: Hunky Dorys, Tayto*

Oliver & Liat Schurmann

Email: schurmann@ireland.com Web: www.mountvenusnursery.com
Tel: +353 (0)86 321 8789 / +353 (0)1 493 3813

2007   **Infinity**
2008   **Twilight** *Sponsor: Homevalue*
2009   **Translucency**
2011   **To The Waters Edge**

Russell Shekleton

& KHS Landscaping Ltd.
Email: info@khs.ie Web: www.khs.ie   Tel: +353 (0)87 410 4611 / +353 (0)46 902 5667

2010   **The Californian Courtyard** *Sponsor: Raisin Eddie, Shamrock Foods*

John Sweeney

Email: vocationaltraining@eve.ie Tel: +353 (0)86 295 9077

2011   **Themae Salute - Wellness Garden**

Lurene Tallon

Email: lurenefitz@msn.com Tel: +353 (0)86 170 9298

2008   **What a Wonderful World We Live in!** (Contractor: Birchall Landscaping)
2009   **The Jewel Garden** *Sponsor of Plants: dyg.ie* (Contractor: Birchall Landscaping)

Rebecca Thorn

Email: designedbyrebecca@gmail.com   Web: www.designedbyrebecca.com
Tel: +353 (0)85 132 9981
2009   Urban Meadow / In Amongst The Grasses

Dale Threadwell

Email: dale@naturallywild.ie   Web: www.naturallywild.ie
Tel: +353 (0)87 977 8803/+353 (0)44 937 9887
2007   AIB Naturally Wild Playgarden *Sponsor:AIB*

Sheena Vernon

Email: sheena@rvalimited.com   Web:www.sheenasgardendesigns.com
Tel: +353 (0)86 321 0600/ +353 (0)1 285 9066
2007   Wake up to Breakfast Garden *Sponsor: Kellogg's*
2008   Awaken the Magic Garden *Sponsor: Kellogg's Coco Pops* (Contractor: Garten Landscapes)
2009   Chic n' Cheerful. Gardening While The Tiger Sleeps
2011   The Lyric FM Garden. Where Life Sounds Better *Sponsor: RTE Lyric FM*
        (Contractor: Michael Corr, Garden Force)

Sophie Von Maltzan

Email: fieldworkandstrategies@gmail.com   Web: www.fieldworkandstrategies.com
Tel: +353 (0)85 703 4201
2009   Recession-Prosperity Garden
2010   For Free
2011   An Outdoor Gallery
2011   The Steam Museum Garden With Robert Guinness
        Sponsor: Steam Museum & Park Lodge Walled Garden

Mark White

Email: mosseyw@gmail.com   Web: www.markwhitelandscapedesign.com
Tel: +353 (0)87 621 0365
2008   An Gairdín Blásta   Salesian College of Horticulture

Simon Williams

Email: swp@iol.ie   Tel: +353 (0)87 923 0056
2007   The Bed of Roses Garden

Orla & Paul Woods

Email: kilmurrynursery@eircom.net   Web: www.kilmurrynursery.com
Tel: +353 (0)86 8180623 / +353 (0)539 48 0223
2009   Keelings Naturally Fresh Garden *Sponsor: Keelings Naturally Fresh*
2009   Honest 2 Goodness Vegetable Garden *Sponsor: Honest2Goodness*

Estelle Wright

Email: estellewrightdublin@yahoo.co.uk Tel:+353 (0)86 859 8326 / +353 (0)1 295 5412
2009   Seeing Is Believing *Sponsor: CFE Dundrum*

Students of Garden Design from	Web: www.scdl.ie Tel: +353 (0)1 280 0385		
Senior College Dun Laoghaire	2007	The Garden That Nobody Saw	By Paul Cox with Sean Prior, Willie Brennan, Eric Molloy, Finn Cremins, Hazeril Mohktar, Keith Keegan and Barry Murphy
	2009	Meadow Labyrinth	By Adrian Eggers & Class
	2010	Patterns of Change	
		. . . A Window to the Future	With Ronnie Nevin

Students of the College of	Email: monicaalvarez@cfedundrum.ie Tel: +353 (0)86 100 3207/+353(0)1 295 5412		
Further Education Dundrum	2009	Seeing Is Believing	Designer: Estelle Wright
	2009	5x5 In The City	Designers: Marion Keogh, Bernie Torpey, Una Thomas
	2011	Columbarium	Designer: Brian Cleary

Rachel Freeman with Staff	Email: Rachel.freeman@itb.ie Web: www.itb.ie Tel: +353 (0)1 8851000	
& Students of the Institute	2011	Out Of The Ruins; A Garden Springs Forth
of Technology Blanchardstown		*Sponsor: Institute of Technology Blanchardstown*

Further Information:

If you require additional information on garden design services, contact the Garden & Landscape Designers Association. (www.glda.ie) the Association of Landscape Contractors of Ireland (www.alci.ie) or the Irish Landscape Institute (www.irishlandscapeinstitute.com).

Bord Bia has additional information on gardening at www.bordbia.ie/gardentime.

Further information on Bloom is available from the website www.bloominthepark.com

Professional Photographers Contact Details:

Koraley Northen	Email: lkn@eircom.net Tel: +353 (0)86 603 9736
Gary O'Neill	Email: info@garyoneillphotography.com Web: www.garyoneillphotography.com Tel: +353 (0)1 454 6184/ +353 (0)87 797 4300
Nick Bradshaw	Email: info@fotonic.ie Web: www.fotonic.ie Tel: +353 (0)87 9208260
David O'Shea	Email: david@osheaphotography.com Web: www.osheaphotography.com Tel: +353 (0)1 839 1259/ +353 (0)87 257 7042
Therese Aherne	Email: info@thereseahernephotography.com Web: www.thereseahernephotography.com Tel: +353 (0)86 803 5430

Acknowledgements

With Thanks to:

The hard working Bloom team in Bord Bia and the event management company and contractors who design and build the Bloom village.

A special thanks to Louise McLoughlin who manages the show gardens with meticulous attention to detail.

Also, special thanks to the four internationally-recognised garden design and horticulture experts who have assessed and judged Bloom's show gardens since 2007. Their guidance has helped to hone the skills of every designer competing at Bloom. They are Andrew Wilson, Paul Maher, Karen Foley and Mark Gregory. The support of guest judges Mary Reynolds and Feargus McGarvey is also acknowledged.

The Bloom show is held on a magnificent 70 acre site in the Visitors Centre, Phoenix Park, Dublin which is managed by the OPW and made available to Bord Bia and Bloom for the 6 weeks each year for the construction and de-rigging of the show.

The continued enthusiasm and commitment of the Irish garden design and construction sector along with Irish nurseries, garden centres, DIYs and allied trades.

All the sponsors, investors and promoters who have helped bring Bloom's show gardens to the public.

All at creative agency, IDEA who have helped in the development of the Bloom brand and their brand guardianship and communication of that brand message.

Finally, the spouses and children of Gary Graham (Anne, Geoff, Izzy and Ellen) and Ciaran Flanagan (Hilary, Angela, Olivia and Gloria) who were neglected for numerous weekends and late nights while this book was being researched, written and designed.

Please Note:

Due to space limitations it was not possible to include a photo of every one of the 142 gardens that featured at Bloom over the past five years. If there is sufficient demand for the publication of a second collection of images this deficiency will be addressed. Please note that the photography that was chosen for use in the book is not a reflection of the standards of achievement or medals awarded to gardens at the Bloom show.

Every care was taken in the preparation of this book to correctly identify plants, designers and photographer credits. We apologize for any error or misrepresentation that we may have overlooked in the final proofing of this publication.

The opinions expressed in this book are those of the authors and do not necessarily represent those of Bord Bia, the garden designers, Bloom judges or garden sponsors.